I0011990

SAMSUNG GALAXY

RING

USER GUIDE

A Complete Step-By-Step Manual To Master And Unlock The New Features Of The Samsung Galaxy Ring, Along With Tips And Tricks.

By

Williams M. Brown

Table of Contents

INTRODUCTION

It's unusual for a major tech firm like Samsung to introduce a whole new market segment. Devices like smartphones, tablets, smartwatches, etc., tend to get the same incremental upgrades somewhat often. But that is no longer the case thanks to the Samsung Galaxy Ring.

While Oura has been the undisputed leader in the smart ring industry for the last many years, Samsung has finally broken into the space with its brand-new Galaxy Ring.

SAMSUNG GALAXY RING: PRICE

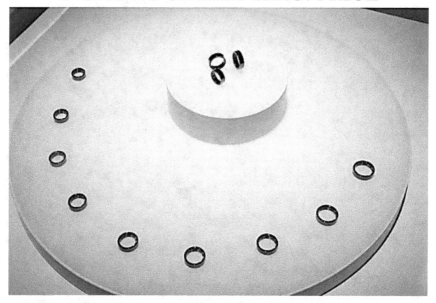

While the Galaxy Ring is Samsung's tiniest offering, it certainly isn't cheap. At $400, you can own the Galaxy Ring.

Despite the Galaxy Ring's fairly high initial cost, it's worth noting that, in contrast to its main rival, Oura, the Galaxy Ring does not need a monthly charge to be used. As an example, the Oura Ring begins at around $299, and a $6/month membership is required to gain any real benefit from it.

Since the Galaxy Ring is a one-time investment, its $400 price tag may end up being less expensive than expected.

SAMSUNG GALAXY RING: RELEASE DATE

Starting on July 10, you may preorder the Galaxy Ring. On July 24, it will be accessible to the general public.

Various merchants, including Samsung Experience Stores, as well as Samsung.com, offer Galaxy Rings for sale. To make sure you get the right size Galaxy Ring for your finger, Samsung includes a free sizing kit with every online purchase.

SAMSUNG GALAXY RING: SPECS

	Samsung Galaxy Ring
Color	Titanium Black (matte) Titanium Silver (matte) Titanium Gold (glossy)
Dimensions	7.0 x 2.6mm
Weight	2.3 grams (Size 5) to 3.0 grams (Size 13)
Sizing	9 (Sizes 5-13)
Memory	8MB
Battery	18mAh (Size 5) to 23.5mAh (Size 13) Charging case: 361mAh
Battery life	6 days (Size 5-11) 7 days (Sizes 12-13)
Charging time	80 minutes
Sensors	Accelerometer PPG Skin temperature
Connectivity	BLE 5.4
Durability	10 ATM IP68 Titanium Grade 5
Price	$400
Subscription	No

SAMSUNG GALAXY RING: DESIGN

The Galaxy Ring is an intelligent ring that is made to be worn all the time, thus its design prioritizes comfort.

The Galaxy Ring from Samsung is remarkably light, weighing just 2.3 to 3.0 grams (ring size dependent) because of its distinctive concave form and construction from Grade 5 Titanium. With a mere 7mm width and 2.6mm thickness, the Galaxy Ring is incredibly thin. It is also water resistant to up to 10 ATMs and has an IP68 certification. From size 5 to 13, you may find the Galaxy Ring.

Titanium Black, Titanium Silver, and Titanium Gold are the three color options available for the Galaxy

Ring, yet there is only one design/shape. The gold has a glossy sheen, but the black and silver are matte.

For the Galaxy Ring, Samsung offers a transparent, multi-purpose charging cover with LED lighting.

SAMSUNG GALAXY RING: HEALTH AND FITNESS TRACKING

Despite its small size, the Galaxy Ring has an array of vital signs monitors. Wearable sensors can monitor vitals like heart rate and sleep.

The Galaxy Ring has a live heart rate monitor and may notify you of dangerously high or low heart rates. With five features—sleep latency, duration in bed, nighttime movement, heart rate, and respiration rate—it boasts Samsung's "best in class" sleep monitoring.

The Samsung Health app is where you can get all of the health data that the Galaxy Ring records. A new sleep AI system from Samsung can analyze your snoring and provide you with a Sleep Score every day. Like the Oura Ring, the Sleep Score may help you learn more about your sleep habits and how to improve them.

An Energy Score is also available, driven by AI. Based on your physical status and well-being across four factors—Sleep, Activity, Sleeping Heart Rate, and Sleeping Heart Rate Variability—this helps you become more aware of how your health affects your everyday life and gives suggestions.

By monitoring your core temperature throughout the night, Cycle Tracking makes it easy to keep tabs on when your period is due. Automatic workout identification is available on the Galaxy Ring as well, although it is presently only able to identify very simple exercises like walking and running.

The Galaxy Ring lacks an electrocardiogram (ECG) and a blood oxygen saturation (BIA) sensor, which means it cannot detect sleep apnea or alert the user to an abnormal heart rate at this time. You should check out the Samsung Galaxy Watch 7 or the Samsung Galaxy Watch Ultra if those features are essential to you.

SAMSUNG GALAXY RING: PERFORMANCE AND BATTERY

Not only does the Galaxy Ring monitor your health and fitness, but it also boasts several additional functions that set it apart from the competition.

If you own a Samsung smartphone, you can use the Galaxy Ring to control your phone using gestures. A double pinch motion, for instance, may snap pictures or silence an alert. When used with a non-Samsung smartphone, such motions will not function on the Galaxy Ring. Although it works with any finger, Samsung suggests the index finger as the best for using the Galaxy Ring's movements.

The 361mAh battery is housed in a see-through charging container. You can see the charging state via the LED lights. But keep an eye on your environment when charging since the charging case does not have an IP certification. With an 18mAh battery, sizes 5–11 last around six days, while sizes 12–13 get seven days (with a bigger 23.5mAh battery). It takes around 80 minutes for a complete charge to get from zero to one hundred percent.

Using the information gathered by both the Galaxy Ring and the Galaxy Watch, Samsung Health will determine which device is more accurate and readable. If it finds that a certain exercise is best performed on the Galaxy Watch, it may switch off certain of the Galaxy Ring's sensors, which can save battery life by up to 30%.

SAMSUNG GALAXY RING: ADDITIONAL FUNCTIONS AND DEVICE COMPATIBILITY

If you ever lose your Samsung Galaxy Ring, don't worry—you can find it with the Samsung Find app. By remembering the last known location of your Galaxy Ring concerning your Galaxy smartphone, Samsung's Find My Ring function makes it easy to find your lost Galaxy Ring. There is no vibration motor or audio feedback on the Galaxy Ring, but it may flash green and red to assist you in identifying it.

Assuming the device can access the Samsung Health app, the Galaxy Ring may be used with any Android smartphone—not limited to Galaxy phones. There is no compatibility for iOS on the Galaxy Ring, which is a major bummer for iPhone owners.

FEATURES OF SAMSUNG GALAXY RING

Sleek, Concave Design

The latest Galaxy shows that tech doesn't have to be cumbersome. The concave design gives Galaxy Ring an elegant twist to its classic style, and the durable titanium frame ensures that it will look great no matter what you do.

Finger-Mounted Tri-Sensor Technology

The technique of one ring with three sensors. Lightweight and comfy, the Galaxy Ring is 7 mm broad, 2.6 mm thick, and 2.3 g, making it an ideal companion for tracking your days and nights.

Optical Bio-signal Sensor

Monitor your heart rate and stay informed of your **heart condition.**

Optical Bio-signal Sensor

Monitor your heart rate and stay informed of your **heart** condition.

Accelerometer

Track the **movements** and **activity** of your body without pressing a button.

Skin Temperature Sensor

Get **regular** readings on how your skin temperature changes while you **sleep.**

Skin Temperature Sensor

Get regular readings on how your skin temperature changes while you sleep.

Powerful Battery With A Maximum Lifespan Of 7 Days

Wearing your Galaxy Ring allows you to travel from work to the gym to bed and back again without worrying about charging the battery. The battery life of the Galaxy Ring is an impressive seven days on a single charge, allowing it to function continuously.

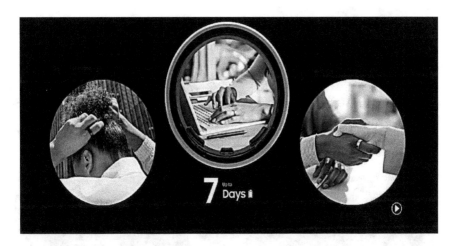

A Wearable Health Tracker Powered By AI

Your Galaxy Ring will gain intelligence as you wear it more often. Just pop the Galaxy Ring onto your finger and it will monitor your vitals continuously. After that, you can see the in-depth health report that Galaxy AI generated by using the Samsung Health app.

Crystal-Clear, Functional Charging Case

The Galaxy Ring remains aesthetically pleasing even as it is charging inside its transparent Charging

Case. The Multi-purpose button's subtle illumination shows the current battery charge level. When you're out and about, just pop your Galaxy Ring into its charging case and set it on a wireless charging pad; the case can also charge your device wirelessly.

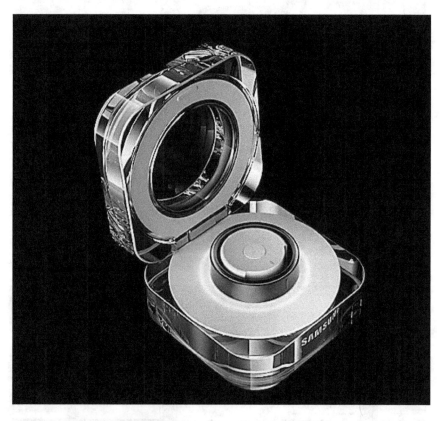

Thin And Feathery.

Great For Both Day And Night

You won't even notice the Galaxy Ring is there because of its thin design and lightweight titanium frame; it's that comfy whether you're cooking, sleeping, or working on a keyboard.

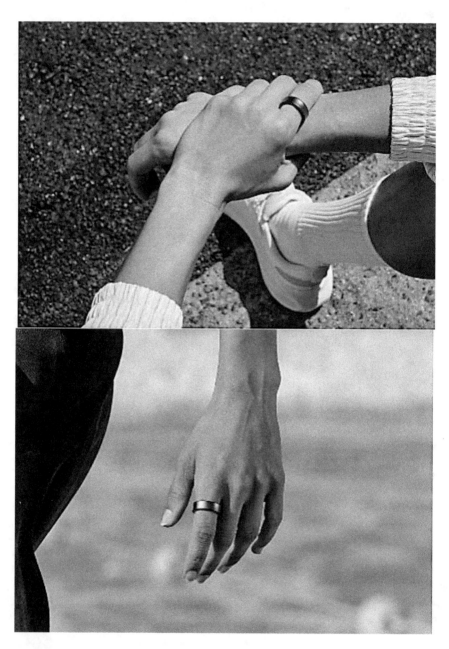

Colors That Match Any Style

Wear the Galaxy Ring wherever you go, from the gym to a formal event. Galaxy Ring complements every outfit, whether you're going for a sleek, sophisticated appearance in Titanium Black or Titanium Silver or a dazzling, golden hue in Titanium Gold. Investigate the Galaxy Ring's three distinct hues in depth.

Rated For Water Resistance At 10 ATM

Whether you're washing your hands, jumping in the shower, or swimming in the ocean, be sure to keep your Galaxy Ring on. Even if you get your Galaxy Ring wet, it will still keep tracking your health since it has a water-resistant certification of 10 ATM.

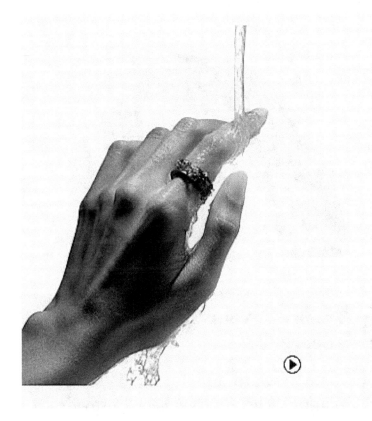

Enhanced Health Insights Provided By AI On Samsung Health

Get a head start on your health journey with insights provided by Galaxy AI on the Samsung Health app. Incorporating Galaxy AI's analysis of your health data into your everyday routine will provide personalized recommendations. If your heart rate seems unstable or if you haven't moved for a long, it will also give you an alarm.

Keep Track Of Your Everyday Health With Energy Score.

The first step toward a better day is being aware of your situation. The Energy Score provides a clear assessment of your health by analyzing your sleep habits, daily activities, and heart rate variability. Use Galaxy AI to plan and make wiser moves.

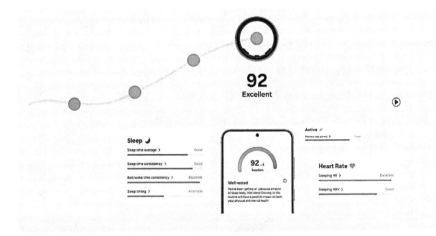

Wellness Tips To Keep You Motivated

Through Wellness Tips, you may get personalized insights. Learn to recognize health trends and get practical guidance on your path to health.

You practiced better sleep habits last week than the week before, averaging a 85% sleep habit achievement rate.
Continue with your sleep coaching to make healthy sleep habits a part of your routine.

52%	85%
Week 2	Last week

Wake Up And Shine With Insights On Improved Sleep

Wearing your Galaxy Ring will help you get a good night's rest. The Galaxy Ring and Samsung Health work in tandem to track your whole night's sleep, including each stage of the cycle, your movements during the night, your core temperature, heart rate variability (HRV), and more. Get data-driven sleep coaching to help you develop more regular sleep patterns.

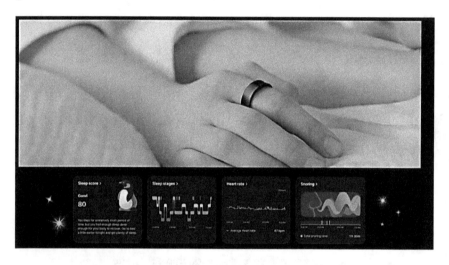

Use Your Skin Temperature To Easily Monitor Your Menstrual Cycles

Galaxy Ring makes it easy to manage your cycles and plan. If your skin temperature changes while you're sleeping, the Skin Temperature Sensor will pick it up. In Cycle Tracking, your next period and the start of your menstrual cycle is predicted using your temperature data by Natural Cycles' modified fertility algorithm.

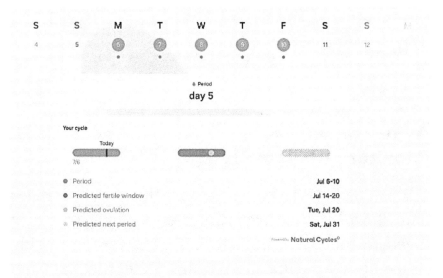

Reliable Heart Rate Monitoring

For calmness' sake, monitor your pulse rate closely. To keep you informed, the Galaxy Ring constantly tracks your heart rate and notifies you via the Samsung Health app if it becomes too high or too low.

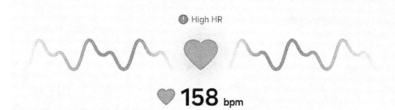

With Galaxy Ring, Your Every Step Is Monitored Automatically.

All you have to do is put Galaxy Ring on your finger, and it will handle everything else. You won't even need to touch a button to get Galaxy Ring to start tracking your runs and walks. Use the Samsung Health app to monitor your progress and see how many calories you've burnt, among other metrics.

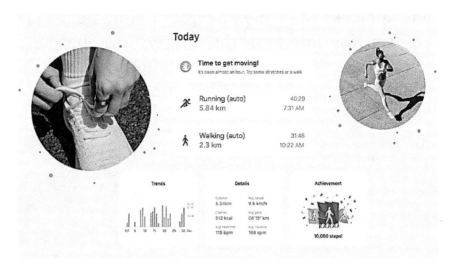

To Manage Your Phone, Just Double-Press The Screen.

Galaxy Ring allows you to operate your associated Samsung Galaxy smartphone with a single gesture, all from the tip of your finger. Snap photos or disable alerts with a simple double-pinch of your thumb and the finger adorned with the Galaxy Ring.

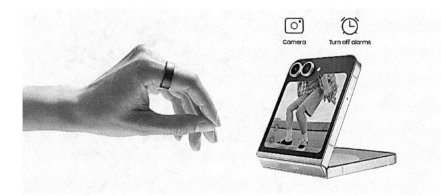

Use Find My Ring To Return To The Previous Spot.

Misplaced your Galaxy Ring? Calm down; using the Find My Ring app on your Samsung Galaxy handset, you can see the last known pairing position of your Galaxy Ring.

CHAPTER ONE

HOW TO USE THE SAMSUNG GALAXY RING

By meticulously monitoring several vital indicators and activity patterns in real-time, the Galaxy Ring aids in health management. At regular intervals, the data collected would be synced with the Samsung Health app.

HOW TO PROPERLY WEAR THE SAMSUNG GALAXY RING

Position the orientation indication face up on your hand when you wear the ring. Pick a finger that's just the right size so the ring doesn't pinch or slip.

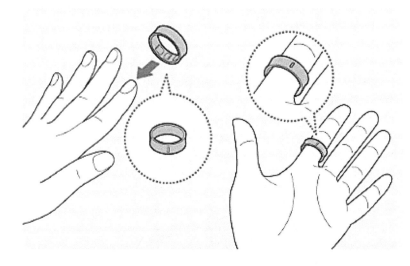

HOW TO CONNECT YOUR RING USING BLUETOOTH

Put your Galaxy Ring in its charging case to make sure it has adequate battery. Please allow the charging case to charge for a minimum of 10 minutes after connecting it to a power source if the battery status indicator does not illuminate. Update the Galaxy Wearables app on your mobile device to the most recent version. The software is available for download on the Galaxy Store.

Step 1

Open the Galaxy Ring charging case. To access the charging case, open it and then hold down the multifunctional function button for three seconds.

Step 2

Select Connect on the mobile device.

Step 3

Press Pair to initiate the Galaxy Ring pairing process.

Step 4

Check the authorizations > Peruse the manual > Select the next option.

In addition to the Galaxy Wearable app, you may connect your Galaxy Ring by going to Settings > Connections > Bluetooth.

CHAPTER TWO

HOW TO CHARGE THE SAMSUNG GALAXY RING BATTERY

A variety of charging options, including cable, wireless, and wireless power sharing, are available for the Galaxy Ring. Put your Galaxy Ring in its charging case to make sure it has enough battery. If the inner band's battery status light isn't lighting up, try plugging the charging case into an electrical outlet and waiting 10 minutes. You may begin using your Ring after it is charged. Before inserting the Ring into the charging case, make sure its orientation indication is in line with the marking on the ring holder of the case.

The Galaxy Ring may be wirelessly charged in three different ways:

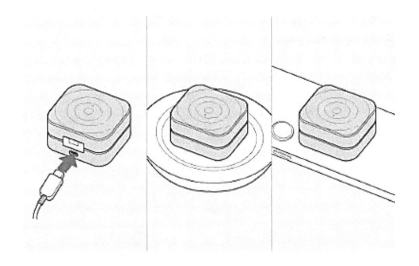

Checking Battery Level

The indicator light on the charging case or the battery status light on the Ring lets you see the current charging state and the amount of battery life left on the device. When you take the Ring off your finger, you can see the battery life indicator.

Light-Detecting Ring

There is a battery level of 15% or more when the green light blinks.

Not charging: Red light blinking

Pressing the Multipurpose button on the charging case will show you the remaining battery level on the indicator light. This may be done while the Ring is in the charging case.

- Check the battery life of your Ring using the Galaxy Wearable app if it's synced with your phone.

Battery Light Identification

Lighting	Status
All lights flash and turn off	Welcome lighting when you open the charging case
Flashes clockwise in sequence	Display the remaining battery level
Flashes clockwise in sequence and blinks at the end	Charging (lighting indicates the remaining battery level)
All lights flash	Fully charged
All lights blink	Charging error
Spins clockwise continuously	Bluetooth pairing mode

SAMSUNG RING MEASUREMENT AND USEFUL FEATURES

The Ring's status, including the connection status, remaining battery level, and recorded health data, can be seen using the Galaxy Wearable app.

Notes:

- Connected phone type, provider, country, and model determine which functions are accessible and which are not.
- Use the button to see all of the devices that are now connected as well as those that have been linked in the past.
- You shouldn't use this function for any kind of medical diagnosis, treatment, or prevention; it's just for your overall health and fitness.

Energy Assessment

Get tips for a healthy, balanced lifestyle and see your energy score derived from an in-depth analysis of the data collected by your Ring, which includes your heart rate, activity level, and sleep.

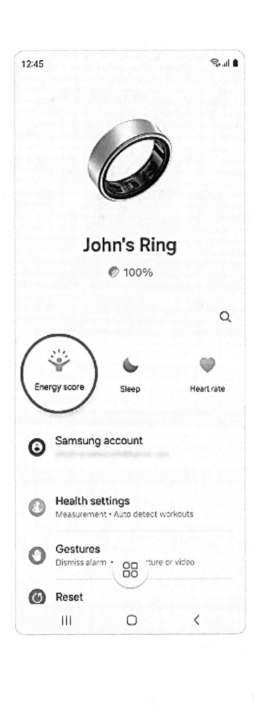

12:45

John's Ring

⬤ 100%

🔍

Energy score   Sleep   Heart rate

⊖ **Samsung account**

🟢 **Health settings**
Measurement • Auto detect workouts

🟢 **Gestures**
Dismiss alarm • ⊞ ~ture or video

⟳ **Reset**

||| ○   ‹

Launch the Galaxy Wearable app. Select Energy index > Take a look at everything that's shown on the screen about your measured Energy score.

Sleep

Your Ring tracks your vitals while you sleep, including your heart rate, blood oxygen levels, and skin temperature, among other metrics.

- Verify the processes:

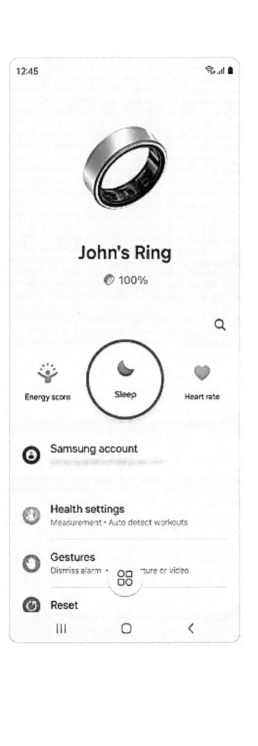

12:45

John's Ring

🔋 100%

Energy score   Sleep   Heart rate

Samsung account

Health settings
Measurement · Auto detect workouts

Gestures
Dismiss alarm · ⋯ture or video

Reset

Launch the Galaxy Wearable app. Select "Sleep" from the menu. Verify every detail about your recorded sleep time on the screen.

- Settings for sleep monitoring on the Galaxy Ring dashboard:

Step 1

Launch the Galaxy Wearable app. Then, go to the Health section and tap on it.

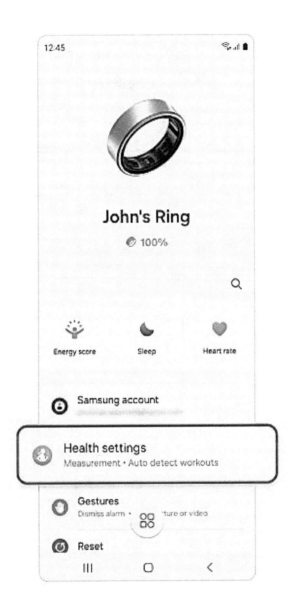

Step 2

Hit the "Sleep" indicator.

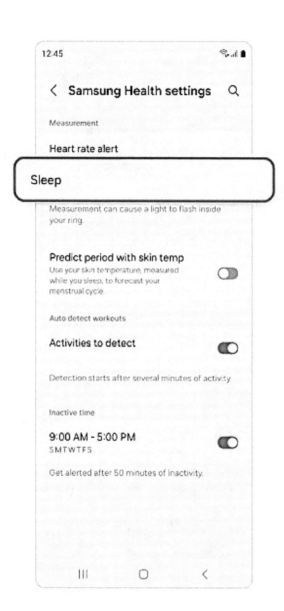

Step 3

Adjust the measurement parameters according to your liking.

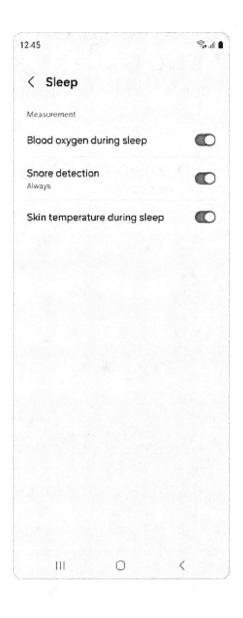

CHAPTER THREE

HOW TO TRACK HEART RATE ON SAMSUNG GALAXY RING

Keep track of your heart rate by measuring it.

Step 1

Launch the Galaxy Wearable app. Then, go to the Health section and tap on it.

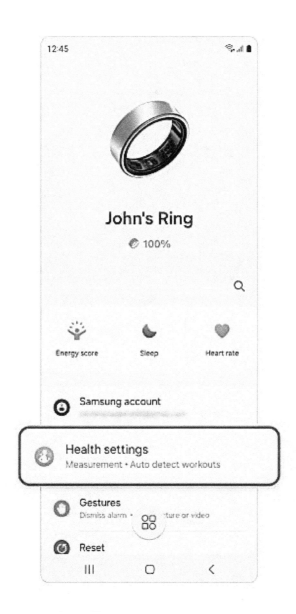

Step 2

Press the heart rate alarm button.

Step 3

Personalize the warnings for a high or low heart rate.

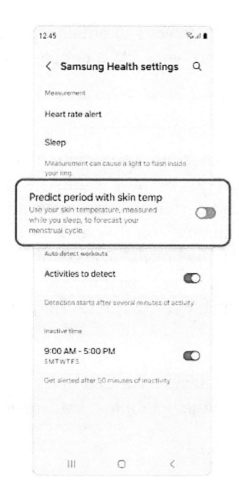

12:45

< Samsung Health settings   Q

Measurement

Heart rate alert

Sleep

Measurement can cause a light to flash inside your ring.

Predict period with skin temp

Use your skin temperature, measured while you sleep, to forecast your menstrual cycle.

Auto-detect workouts

Activities to detect

Detection starts after several minutes of activity

Inactive time

9:00 AM - 5:00 PM
SMTWTFS

Get alerted after 50 minutes of inactivity

HOW TO TRACK YOUR MENSTRUAL CYCLE USING THE SAMSUNG GALAXY RING

Your Ring can detect and anticipate your menstrual cycle by taking your skin temperature while you sleep.

Notes:

- The dates of ovulation that have been predicted are only estimates and may not match up with the real dates. Do not use the information for diagnosing, treating, or preventing any medical condition.
- You should not use the monitoring tool to plan a pregnancy or to contracept yourself.

Step 1

Go to the Galaxy Wearable app's health settings. Then, choose the option to "Predict period with skin temp."

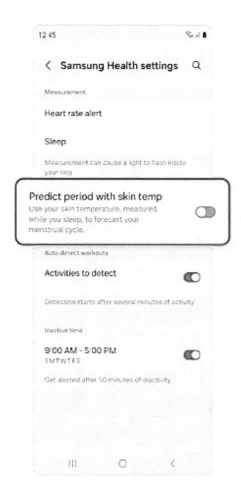

Step 2

Confirm the beginning and ending dates of your most recent billing cycle. Select the next option.

Step 3

Choose the duration of the cycle, and then hit the "Done" button.

Step 4

Turn on the "Predict period with skin temp" feature once you've agreed to the disclaimer.

12:45

< Samsung Health settings   Q

Measurement

Heart rate alert

Sleep

Measurement can cause a light to flash inside
your ring.

Predict period with skin temp
Use your skin temperature, measured
while you sleep, to forecast your
menstrual cycle.

Auto detect workouts

Activities to detect

Detection starts after several minutes of activity.

Inactive time

9:00 AM - 5:00 PM
SMTWTFS

Get alerted after 50 minutes of inactivity.

CHAPTER FOUR

HOW TO USE THE ACTIVITY MONITOR ON SAMSUNG GALAXY RING

The Galaxy Ring will begin tracking your workouts automatically once a certain amount of time has passed of constant use. Wearing your ring allows you to track a variety of activity metrics, including steps, exercise duration, and calories burnt during and after exercise. The Samsung Health app makes it easy to see all diagnostics.

- Get auto detect set up:

Step 1

Launch the Galaxy Wearable app and then go to the Health section.

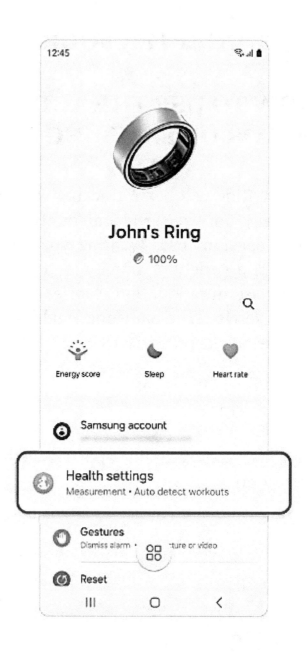

Step 2

Choose "Activities to detect," then "Turn switch On." Then, choose the actions you want the app to recognize automatically.

12:45

< **Auto detect workouts**

On ⬤

Activities to detect

Walking
Record location off ⬤

Running ⬜

Note: The accuracy of the measurements could be affected by factors such as the way you walk, the exercises you do, and your overall lifestyle.

Stress Monitor

You may monitor your stress levels using the biodata that your Ring collects. With the Samsung Health app, you can see your stress levels and see your breathing exercises.

NOTIFICATIONS AND TROUBLESHOOTING FOR SAMSUNG GALAXY RING
Things To Keep In Mind When Using Your Galaxy Ring

- Even when going about your daily routine, your ring might get scratches or nicks if you aren't attentive. Carefully handle your ring, since they are not covered by the guarantee.
- On the hand that you don't use very often, wear your ring.
- Keep your metal ring finger or finger rings from touching.
- When you're dealing with heavy or tough things, take off your Ring.
- To avoid injuring your hand, do not wear your Ring when exercising on machines. This is particularly true when using weights,

dumbbells, or iron bars since they are bar-like objects.

- While wearing this ring, please use caution while touching other items, such as phones, phone cases, watches, etc.
- Wearing the ring on one hand while holding a magnet or other magnetic item on the other can cause certain features, such as step counting, to malfunction.
- Before you put on the ring, make sure your finger and it are both dry.
- Please discontinue wearing the ring and seek medical attention if it causes any skin irritation.
- To avoid irreparable harm to the sensors, refrain from cleaning the gadget using an ultrasonic cleaner.
- The storage cradle for the Ring has rubber pads attached to it so that it does not slide about when mounted. When the Ring is kept for an extended length of time, the rubber pads that contact the inner band may develop small indentations. In terms of the Ring's practical performance, this is irrelevant.

In case of an emergency, if you must remove the Ring, do so along its orientation indication so as not to harm its battery.

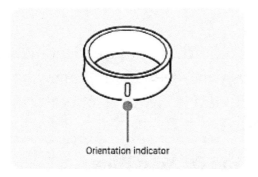

Orientation indicator

CHAPTER FIVE

TIPS AND TRICKS

1. Sleep

At the same time that you are sleeping, Sleep Your Ring analyzes your sleep by tracking your heart rate, blood oxygen levels, skin temperature, and other characteristics.

2. Tracking Of Activities

After a certain amount of time has passed during which the Galaxy Ring has been constantly used for physical activity, it will automatically recognize the activity and begin recording it. Your ring will record activity diagnostics such as the number of steps you take, the amount of time you spend exercising, and the total number of calories you burn. A comprehensive picture of all tests is available via the Samsung Health app.

3. Stress Monitor

Using the biodata that your Ring has acquired, you can determine how much stress you are experiencing. By utilizing the Samsung Health app, one can monitor their stress levels as well as their breathing exercises.

4. Monitoring Of The Menstrual Cycle

Your menstrual cycle may be tracked and predicted with the help of your Ring via the measurement of your skin temperature while you are sleeping.

www.ingramcontent.com/pod-product-compliance
Lightning Source LLC
LaVergne TN
LVHW051613050326
832903LV00033B/4479

* 9 7 9 8 3 3 3 6 4 0 4 8 2 *